Spiritual Meaning of

Aromas, Colors,

Flowers & Trees

Compiled by Kathie Walters
&
Bob Jones

Mrs. Crystal I. Moore
2129 Kristen's Channel
Florence, SC 29501

International Standard Book Number:
978-1-888081-94-7

Published by

GOOD NEWS FELLOWSHIP MINISTRIES
220 Sleepy Creek Road
Macon, GA 31210
Phone: (478) 757-8071

E-mail: goodnewsministries@usa.com
www.KathieWaltersMinistry.com

Table of Contents

Note from Kathie Walters

Many times in a meeting, service, or just in a normal day, a scent or aroma can be smelled that does not have a natural origin (like smelling roses in a rose garden.) So when the aroma comes out of the blue, so to speak, this is usually the Lord manifesting His presence and speaking something to us.

It is a key to understand what these aromas mean, so that we may then understand what it is the Lord is saying to us. He speaks in many different ways. All manifestations of the Spirit are God speaking something to us. We should always stop and ask the Lord what He is saying when we see various manifestations of the Spirit.

This is a list of those most common aromas we have come across. Most of the time, these aromas have a particular meaning, but please be sure to seek the Holy Spirit for yourself. Though usually this list could be used to interpret the meanings, be sensitive to the witness inside you, because this list is not set it in stone. It is a guide to help you further understand the many wondrous ways in which the Lord speaks. Kathie Walters compiled this list with Bob Jones.

Many thanks to my "ducky" prophetic friends for their help and of course poppa Bob Jones who has always helped me understand things that were happening to me, in me and around me,

The lists of Colors, Flowers & Trees are compiled by Kathie Walters. These are the most agreed upon interpretations among many scholars and ministries. The aroma of a certain fruit is not necessarily the same as the meaning of the tree itself.

MEANING OF AROMAS

Alcohol -Usually means someone needs deliverance from alcoholism.

Aloe -Healing and/or comfort. The Lord is bringing healing/comfort.

.

Almonds - Authority, God's choice. Aaron's rod that blossomed **(Numbers11)** Jeremiah saw the rod of an Almond tree **(Jeremiah 1)**

Amber - The Heavenly throne, invitation from God

Ammonia - Cleansing. Cleansing the heart or spirit

Ants - Blazing new trails. Also can be wisdom, strength or warning against folly **(Proverbs 6 & 30)**

Apples - Beloved's breath smells like sweet apples; freedom **(Song of Sol 7)**

Ashes - Offering or sacrifice burnt up and now clean **(Leviticus and Numbers)**. Could also be mourning **(Isaiah 61, Psalms 102, Job)**

Baby Powder - Comfort, Soothing, Softening. New Christians

Bananas – Gentleness

Barbeque - Meat: Rhema word, deeper things of God **(Hebrews 5)**

Barley - Harvest. Can be harvest of souls or harvest of righteousness

Blackberry – Cleansing.

Bread - Fresh word; Jesus is the Bread of Life
(John 6)

Bubble Gum - Being childlike

Buckwheat - Childlike: The little rascals (term of endearment). Having fun. Also buckwheat is a highly versatile and healthy food item.

Burning-(good) Fire of God

Burning -(bad) Enemy leading to wrong direction

Butterscotch - Sweet perfect oil

Campfire - Counsel of God; Wisdom. Hang out with God

Carnations – Wedding

Cassia - Fragrance of Jesus, closely related to cinnamon.

Cat Pee - Wrong plan or lasciviousness. Can also be territorial.

Cedar - Incorruptible, Royalty

Cherries – Balm. Cherry has pain reducing and anti-inflammatory qualities.

Chocolate - Sweet spirit

Cigar - Like grandfathers cigar. Could be grandfather in the natural or in the spiritual. There are many spiritual grandfathers.

Cigarette Smoke - usually someone needs deliverance from addiction

Cinnamon - Fragrance of creation, closely related to Cassia

Cleaners – Lysol etc. Cleansing from spirits, or wrong thoughts

Cloves - Taste for God, also warming and pain killer

Coconut - Good teaching; milk and meat together.

Coffee - Wake up!

Cookies - Heavenly Manna

Cotton Candy - Cotton candy comes at the end of the fair. At the end of something; a treat at the finish of a meeting, teaching etc. Lifts weights from the mind.

Cumin - Seeds of truth

Dirt - Flesh (dust, **Genesis 2:7**)

Dog Pee - Territorial spirit

Disinfectant - Cleansing from spirits, bad thought patterns

We're gonna—
Rise Up & Take Action when we
do. that's when the whole
atmosphere shifts—

That's why we said—"That's a
terrible idea, what time?"

We're gonna Show up in places
where people need to hear—

But there gonna hear the way
they can listen—

And we're Gonna Speak the way that
they hear—So we can be effective

Lance—Peanut Bar

effective.

Dog - Religious spirit

Dog (wet) - Homosexual spirit

Eggs - New life, new seed planted. Seed could be a word, dream, calling, gifting etc.

Eggs (rotten) - A seed that has gone bad

Eucalyptus - Medicine, cleaning, deodorizing, decongestant. Sometimes comes with laughter (laughter is the best medicine)

Figs - Self effort

Fir (like Christmas tree) – Presents. Childlike

Fish - Grace. The sign of the early Christian.

Fish (bad) - False prophesy

Flowers - The heavenly realm Specific flower see Flowers list

Fly Spray - Satan is the lord of the flies. Flies are often lies. Counteract with truth. Truth kills lies.

Frankincense - Portal into heaven is open. More of God

Garlic - Cleanses and brings health. Means healthy

Gardenia - A wedding flower.

Gingerbread - The Word (or a word) made palatable

Gold (taste) – Heavenly. See also colors section

Grapes – Loyal

Grapefruit - Self control; Staying focused

Grass – Fading

Green Plants - New life. New growth

Hair spray - Trying to keep reputation. Keep things in place. Someone needs to let go

Herbs - Words from God to heal

Honey - Revelation **(1 Samuel 14)**

Honeysuckle – Praise

Horses-Flesh, power of man

Horses (sound) - Prepare for war

Ink -Writing

Jasmine - Deep love

Lavender – Purity

Leather - New wineskin being made or needed, Luxury

Leeks - Fruit from the world

Lemons – Refreshing

Lilac - Lover, aroma from your heart to the Lord

Lilies – Intercession

Lily of the Valley - Holy Clothing, Jesus, righteousness

Limes - Refreshing and flavor enhancer

Licorice - Breath freshener, cleanser. Having to do with Praise coming out of the mouth

Maple Syrup – Awakening

Meat - Mature word

Meat (rotting) - Word/truth distorted, not fresh, not clean

Metal (taste) – Discernment

Milk (warm) - Getting ready to receive, the milk of the word.

Milk (sour) - Turning sour on life, souring word.

Mold - Something old - no longer relevant. Ripeness turns to rottenness if not eaten at the right time.

Mothballs - Preservative, ancient mantles and anointings that have been stored away.

Musk – Conception

Mustard -Small beginning but grows large Real faith involved. Faith of a mustard seed can move mountains.

Myrrh - Washing away pride, vanity.

Myrtle – Beauty

Nursing Home Smell - Stuck in a place, time to move on

Ocean - Restless, moving

Oil - Anointing of the Lord

Oil (rancid) - Anointing that has gone stale (religious)

Olives - Anointing (having to do with Israel)

Oak - Righteousness, spiritual relationship

Onions - Good things of Egypt, but not the promised land.

Oranges - Love, sweet companionship of the Lord

Oriental Spices - Caution; eastern, false light spirit

Palm – Faithful

Peaches - Joy, sense of well being. God loves me

Pear – Patience

Pee (urine) - Cleansing out the old, renewing a right spirit. Territorial

Pencil Shavings – Writing

Peppermint – Refreshing

Peppers - Bringing deliverance

Perfume (stale) - Religious spirit

Pine Tree - Grows in the sun, is a high and lofty tree. Stand for high vision- able to see

Pineapple - Balance, staying in the Spirit all the time

Poop (human) - Mystic, false prophesy

Popcorn - Break out, explosions of God. Promises are bursting forth

Rain - Refreshes, waters. Can be blessing or teaching

Rats - Works of the mind, an abomination

Roast Beef - Maturity of word or spirit

Roses - Jesus sweetheart. Lover of our soul.

Sea – Humanity

Shoe Polish - Get ready to go

Smoke - Prayers going up like incense to the Lord

Soap – Cleansing

Sour milk - Turning sour on circumstances or life. Wrong teaching or teaching that comes from bitter spirit

Spikenard - Prayer and praise as incense unto the Lord

Strawberries -Friendship with God, Healing.

Sweet Potatoes - Lowly potato. Humility, unity

Sulphur - Demonic power or presence

Tanning oil - Resting in the Spirit, laying out, enjoying basking in His glory.

Toast - Getting slammed by God (toasted)

Tomato - Kindness, generous

Vanilla - (Milk and honey) Pure word and revelation

Water up nose - Cleansing of the mind

Wet Dog - Homosexual spirit

White Shoulders Perfume - Good government

White Linen Perfume-Clothed with His
Righteousness

Wine - Holy Spirit

Woodsmoke - Burning, cleansing, fire of God, Faith

Meaning of Flowers

Allium—Prosperous—Good News

Anemone Flowers - The Trinity, Abandonment to God.

Antirrhinum –Sweet attraction of the Spirit

Astor—New Beginnings

Bachelor's Button– Time alone with God

Bird of Paradise—Strange and Wonderful Acts of God

Buttercup—Childlike Spirit

Camellia- Honest, Excellence

Carnation Flowers - Red carnation symbolizes love, Wedding

Chrysanthemum —Hope

Columbine Flowers - Holy Spirit

Crocus-Youthful. Gladness

Daffodils - New season. Chivalry , Waiting.

Dahlia– Changing

Daisy - Childlike, Happy

Dandelion - Symbolizes Christ's Passion.

Delphinium– Swift and Light.

Dogwood– Endurance

Forget -Me-Not– Keepsake. Eternity

Freesia—Calm. Peaceful

Gardenia-Grace

Gerbera– Purity

Gladiolus- Grace. Sweetness

Heather—Passion

Heliotrope– Devotion

Hibiscus– Opportunities

Hollyhock– Fertile

Honeysuckle– Bonds of Love

Hyacinth - Prudence and peace of mind.

Hydrangea– Reminder to be Humble

Iris Flowers - Brings Message of Hope

Jasmine-Good News, fortune

Lavender and Lilac – English. New Season

Lilac– Beautiful (can also be sadness, but not grief)

Lily - Purity, Innocence

Lily of the Valley - Jesus. Also morning of a new day
or new season

Marigold-Ardent, True

Mimosa– Sensitive, caring

Myrtle - Symbolizes those converted to Christ

Narcissus– Ego

Nasturtium– Laughter. Joy. Funny

Orchid– Ecstasy

Pansy - Remembrance & meditation.

Peony– Hidden

Periwinkle- Promise

Plumeria– Aloha, Love in Presence or Absence

Pomegranate– Unspoken desires

Poppy – Rest. Dreams

Primrose– Youthfulness. Hope

Protea - Desire of the Heart

Queen Anne's Lace– Strong or Self Reliant

Quince-Resist temptation

Ranunculus - Charming, Sweet, Kind, Forgiving

Rose Red– Love

Rose Yellow—Jealousy God is jealous over us

Rose White– Purity and Quietness

Rose- See also aromas section

Rosemary-Remembrance, good memories

Snapdragon– Impetuous.

Sweet Pea-Lasting Pleasure or happiness

Sunflower-Power, warmth, Nourishment

Tulip– Declare. Bold. Love

Violet-Humility. Faithfulness

Wisteria-Gentleness. Obedience.

Water Lily– Perfect, Beauty

Zinnia– Absent. Something or someone missing

Meaning of Trees

Acacia Tree - Purity

Almond Trees -Divine approval (Numbers 17:1-8)

Apple Tree – Beauty, Generosity

Bulrush Plants - Faithfulness and humility

Cedar of Lebanon Trees - Christ, Incorruptible,
Royalty

Cherry Tree- Sweetness and good character

Chestnut Trees - Chastity

Clover Plants - or Shamrock, is a symbol of for the Trinity.

Cyclamen Plants - Purity

Cypress Trees – Death. Sacrifice

Elder Tree - Continuation

Elm Trees - Dignity and faithfulness.

Fern Plants - Humility

Fig - Fertility

Fir Trees - Patience.

Grapes- Blood of Christ

Holly - Christ's crown of thorns and His Passion.

Hyssop- Sorry for sin, Humility and Baptism

Ivy- Faithfulness & eternal life.

Laurel - Victory or triumph and can also symbolize eternity.

Lemon Tree- Fidelity in love. Refresh

Myrtle- Divine Love. Immortality

Oak - Righteousness, spiritual relationship **(Isaiah 61),** Sturdy and strength

Olive Trees- Peace

Orange Tree- Purity, chastity and generosity

Palm - Victory.

Peach Tree- Virtue and Goodness

Pears Tree – Christ's love for Mankind

Pine tree - Grows in the sun, is a high and lofty tree. Stand for high vision- able to see

Plane Tree- Christian love and character

Plantain- Seeking Christ and His kingdom

Plum- Faithfulness and courage

Pomegranate- The Church with many Seeds, Resurrection, Fruitfulness

Poplar Tree – Victory, Transformation, Vision

Reed Plants- Humiliation and is a symbol of Christ's Passion.

Strawberry Bush- Righteousness, Friendship

Silver Birch – Growth, Revival, Transformation

Thistle-Curses

Vine- Christ. God's Providence, Heavenly Care

Wheat- Harvest

Willow Tree – Gospel message. Good News

Meaning of Colors

Amber - God's Glory

Black - Righteous Judgment, Death

Blue - Heavenly Realm, Revelation

Blue (Light) - Heavenly Realm

Blue (Dark) - God's Mandates

Brown – Humanity

Brown (Dark) - Fellowship and Communion

Bronze - Strength of Man

Burgundy - Self Motivated

Coral - Having Value. Deliverance

Cream – Healing

Crystal - Bride of Christ, Holy Spirit

Crimson - Christ Atonement

Emerald - God's Presence. God's Throne

Gold - God's Glory in Power. Divine Nature, Brilliance of God's countenance

Gray - Of the earth

Green - New life, Flourish, Prosper

Green (Light) – Sickness

Lavender – Sorrow

Orange - Praise, Intercession, Boldness

Pearl - Truth and purity

Pink - Friendship with God, Healing

Purple - Royalty, Wealth

Rainbow - God's Promise and Covenant

Red - Blood Covenant

Rose Pink – Caring

Shekinah - God's Presence

Silver - Redemption, Grace of God

White – Holiness

Yellow - Joy, Glory

For a fuller and more complete understanding
of
Colors & Flags for use in Worship
see:

"*Biblical Use of Colors & Flags*"
Sharon Busby
www.flags4worship.com

Kathie ministers in churches, conferences, and woman's conferences. She believes that the realm of the Spirit, the supernatural realm, the angels, miracles etc. are meant to be a normal part of the life of every Christian. The religious spirit prevents Gods people from receiving their inheritance.

She invites you to peruse her many other books and teaching CD's and DVD's on her website. Kathie believes the realm of the Spirit, the Supernatural realm, the Angels, Heavenly visitations are meant to be a normal part of the life of every Christian. We don't have to qualify- Jesus already qualified us 100% when He died and rose again.

Teaching CD's

by Kathie Walters

Getting Free and Living in the Supernatural

In Depth for Seers and Prophets

Spiritual Strategies

The Almond Tree

The Fanatic in the Attic

Faith and Angels

Revival Accounts and Getting your Family Saved

Spiritual Abortion

For further information on

Kathie or David Walters ministry

write or call

Good News Ministries

220 Sleepy Creek Rd.

Macon GA 31210

goodnewsministries@usa.com

(478) 757-8071

http://kathiewaltersministry.com

Books By Kathie Walters

ANGELS WATCHING OVER YOU

Did you know that angels are active in our everyday lives?

THE BRIGHT AND SHINING REVIVAL

An account of the Hebrides Revival 1948–1952.

CELTIC FLAMES

Read the exciting accounts of famous fourth- and fifth century Celtic Christians: Patrick, Brendan, and others.

COLUMBA—THE CELTIC DOVE

Read about the ministry of this famous Celtic Christian, filled with supernatural visitations.

PARENTING BY THE SPIRIT

The author shows how she raised her children by listening to the Holy Spirit rather than her emotions.

LIVING IN THE SUPERNATURAL

How to live in our inheritance—supernaturally.

THE SPIRIT OF FALSE JUDGMENT

In the light of holy revelation, sometimes things are

different from what we perceive them to be.

THE VISITATION

Supernatural visitations of a mother and daughter.

PROGEST...WHAT?

Natural hormone replacement explained.

Books By David Walters

KIDS IN COMBAT

Training children and youth to be radical for God.

For youth and children's pastors and parents.

EQUIPPING THE YOUNGER SAINTS

A guide for teachers and parents on teaching children

about salvation and spiritual gifts.

CHILDREN AFLAME

Amazing accounts of children from the journals of the

great Methodist preacher John Wesley in the 1700's and

David's own accounts with children and youth today.

RADICAL LIVING IN A GODLESS SOCIETY

Our Godless society really targets our children and youth.

How do we cope with this situation?

THE ANOINTING & YOU

Understanding Revival

What we must do to receive and impart the anointing &

revival to pass it on to the next generation.

LIVING IN REVIVAL

The Everyday Lifestyle Of The Normal Christian

God's intention for us through the power of His Holy Spirit. Diary of Miraculous Events, Angelic visitations, freedom of the spirit, Divine encounters, Deliverance, Healing, Prosperity and Salvation.

HOW TO BE ORDINIARY, AVERAGE, MEDIOCRE & UNSUCESSFUL

An amusing reverse psychology booklet that says if you do the opposite to what this booklet proposes you may suffer the curse of being successful.

CHILDREN'S BIBLE STUDY BOOKS
(ILLUSTRATED) FOR AGES 6–15
With Multiple-Choice Questions & Answers

BEING A CHRISTIAN

A Bible study teaching children and teens how to be a Christian.

FACT OR FANTASY?

A study on Christian Apologetics designed for children and youth.

THE ARMOR OF GOD

A children's Bible study based on Ephesians 6:10–18.

CHILDREN'S PRAYER MANUAL

Children's illustrated study on prayer

FRUIT OF THE SPIRIT

A study teaching children and teens how to be a fruitful Christian.

THE GIFTS OF THE SPIRIT

Children's illustrated Bible study on the gifts of the Spirit (ages 7 years–adult).

Adventure Books For Youngsters.

By David Walters.

THE BOOK OF FUNTASTIC ADVENTURES

Bedtime stories to make children & parents laugh Eleven imaginary stories of David's two grandsons as Jedi knights having amazing hilarious adventures with Superheroes & story book characters. Ages 8-14

THE SECOND BOOK OF FUNTASTIC ADVENTURES

More hilarious adventures of David's two grandsons as Jedi Knights traveling through space with Moses their robot pilot searching for their parents and sister who have been kidnapped by aliens.

Ages 8-14

THE ADVENTURES OF TINY THE BEAR

An amusing set of stories to help children deal with name calling and bullying. Ages 6-10

TOURS OF IRELAND AND SCOTLAND

with Kathie Walters

Come to Ireland and Scotland on a 14-Day Celtic Heritage Tour with Kathie Walters!

• Pray on the Hill of Slane where St. Patrick lit his Pascal fire and defied the High King.

• See the place where St. Patrick first landed to bring the Gospel to Ireland by God through the Angel of Ireland, Victor.

• See the green hills and dales of Ireland—a picture you will never forget.

• Visit the ancient places of worship that will help enable you to grasp hold of your godly inheritance.

Then on to Scotland

• Tour the beautiful highlands of Scotland.

• Visit the island of Iona, where St. Columba built his monastery.

See beautiful Loch Ness and Loch Lomond and visit Edinburgh

For further information on

Kathie or David Walters ministry

write or call

Good News Ministries

220 Sleepy Creek Rd.

Macon GA 31210

goodnewsministries@usa.com

(478) 757-8071

http://kathiewaltersministry.com